TELESCOPES

Carla Mooney

Rourke
Educational Media

rourkeeducationalmedia.com

Before & After Reading Activities

Before Reading:

Building Academic Vocabulary and Background Knowledge

Before reading a book, it is important to tap into what your child or students already know about the topic. This will help them develop their vocabulary, increase their reading comprehension, and make connections across the curriculum.

1. *Look at the cover of the book. What will this book be about?*
2. *What do you already know about the topic?*
3. *Let's study the Table of Contents. What will you learn about in the book's chapters?*
4. *What would you like to learn about this topic? Do you think you might learn about it from this book? Why or why not?*
5. *Use a reading journal to write about your knowledge of this topic. Record what you already know about the topic and what you hope to learn about the topic.*
6. *Read the book.*
7. *In your reading journal, record what you learned about the topic and your response to the book.*
8. *After reading the book complete the activities below.*

Content Area Vocabulary
Read the list. What do these words mean?

astronomer
atmosphere
celestial
convex
focal point
infrared
lenses
optical
parabola
reflecting
refracting

After Reading:

Comprehension and Extension Activity

After reading the book, work on the following questions with your child or students in order to check their level of reading comprehension and content mastery.

1. *What are some of the things astronomers study using telescopes? (Summarize)*
2. *How have telescopes helped us learn more about the universe? (Infer)*
3. *How is a refracting telescope different than a reflecting telescope? (Asking questions)*
4. *If you could look into a telescope, what would you like to see? (Text to self connection)*
5. *Why does the Hubble space telescope produce such clear images? (Asking questions)*

Extension Activity

Make A Simple Telescope - Have an adult help you follow the instructions at this site: http://kids.nationalgeographic.com/explore/nature/make-a-telescope/.
Use your telescope to study the night sky. What do you see?

TABLE OF CONTENTS

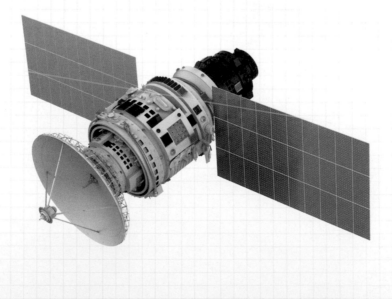

The First Telescopes

Humans have always studied the sky. At first, they used their eyes to view **celestial** objects. It was difficult to see stars and planets so far away. Many remained hidden from sight.

In the early 1600s, Hans Lippershey was a Dutch lens maker. He designed the first practical telescope. A telescope is an **optical** tool. It is used to make objects appear closer. In 1608, Lippershey placed two **lenses** in a tube. When looking through the device, he saw objects appear three times larger.

Hans Lippershey (1570–1619)

After hearing about the Dutch invention, Italian physicist Galileo Galilei built his own telescope. Galileo's telescope used two lenses to concentrate light. A **convex** primary lens curved outward. A concave eyepiece lens curved inward. This delivered more light to the human eye than it could collect alone. The lens refracted the light and formed an image. This type of telescope became known as a **refracting** telescope.

Galileo's telescope could magnify objects 20 times. Still, it was not perfect. The spherical shape of its primary lens made images blurry. Also, the lens split light into many colors. This created a ring of color around a bright image.

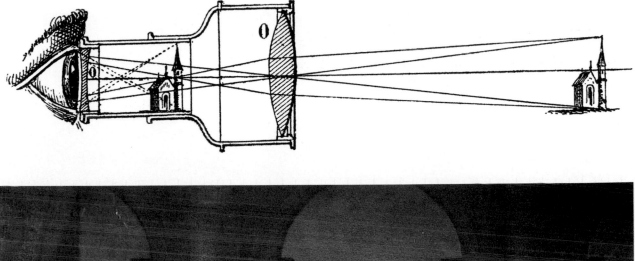

This painting shows Galileo Galilei showing people how to use his telescope to view the night sky.

Galileo became the first person to use a telescope to study the sky. Through his telescope, he could see mountains and craters on the moon. He discovered four large moons around Jupiter. He saw sunspots on the sun. He also saw a ribbon of light across the sky. This was the Milky Way galaxy.

Galileo Galilei was the first person to see the four largest moons of Jupiter — Io, Europa, Ganymede, and Callisto — through his telescope in 1610.

Galileo Galilei

*Galileo Galilei was an Italian mathematician, philosopher, physicist, and **astronomer**. Galileo conducted scientific experiments to test his hypotheses. He is often considered the father of modern science. He is also credited with developing modern astronomy.*

(1564–1642)

Galileo used his telescope to make observations. He drew conclusions about the objects he saw. Galileo's telescope opened the door for astronomy. Astronomy is the study of celestial objects such as the sun, moon, and stars. Since the telescope's invention, knowledge about the universe has grown greatly.

Seasons – Movement of the Earth and Sun

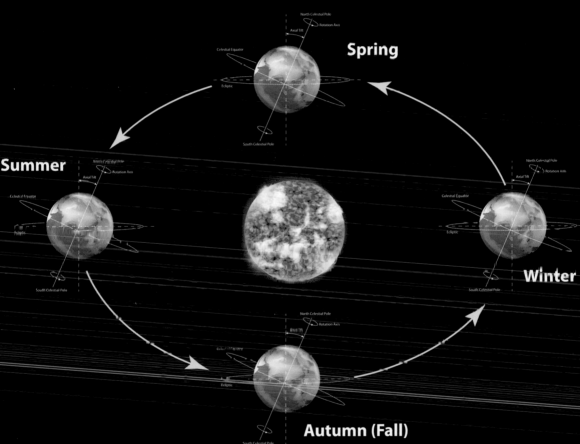

Revolving Around the Sun
Before Galileo's telescope, many people believed the sun revolved around the Earth. Galileo's discoveries proved the Earth and other planets revolved around the sun.

Refracting Telescopes

The first telescopes were refracting telescopes. Refraction happens when light passes through different substances, such as air and glass. The different densities of the two substances cause the light to bend.

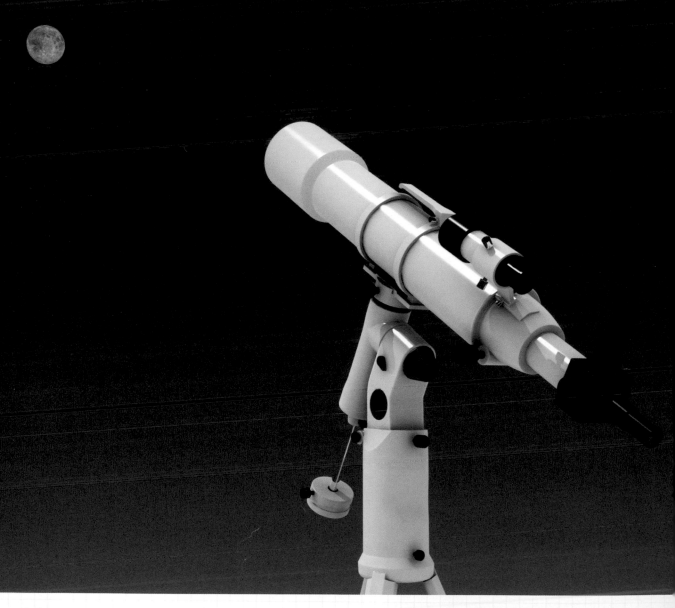

Refracting Telescope

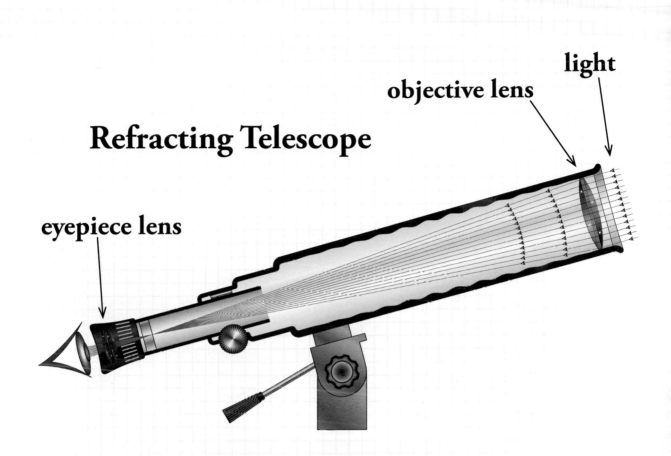

eyepiece lens

objective lens

light

Light enters a refracting telescope through its objective lens. This lens bends incoming light rays. The rays meet at a **focal point** in the telescope.

The light travels down the telescope to the eyepiece lens. The eyepiece lens makes the light rays parallel again. This magnifies the object. It makes the object appear closer than it is.

The first refracting telescopes were small. The focal length was only a few feet long. The focal length is the distance between the center of a lens and the focal point, where the parallel rays of light meet.

Kepler's Telescope

Around 1611, astronomer Johannes Kepler built a refracting telescope with two convex lenses. A convex lens has a center that is thicker than its edges. It made the images appear upside down. At the same time, it also made them clearer. Using a convex lens also widened the telescope's field of view. It allowed the viewer to see a much larger area.

Johannes Kepler (1571–1630)

In the mid-1600s, scientists discovered the flatter the telescope's objective lens, the longer light rays had to travel before they focused. This produced a clearer image. It also increased the telescope's focal length. The telescope's two lenses had to be placed farther apart.

Kepler's design for an Improved Refractor

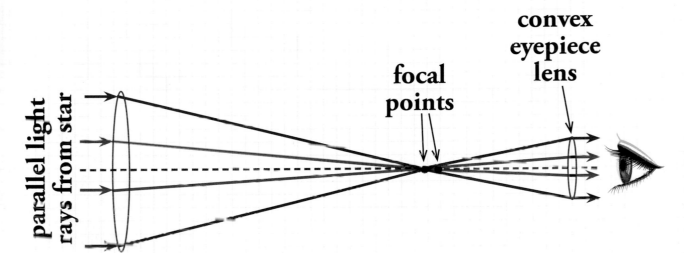

parallel light rays from star

focal points

convex eyepiece lens

a less-curved primary lens

In Kepler's telescope design, a flatter primary lens focuses light rays at closer focal points. This makes the image being viewed much clearer.

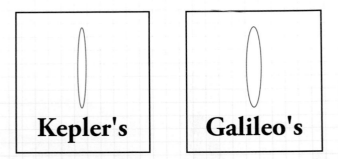

Kepler's   **Galileo's**

Using this idea, astronomers built longer telescopes. Some telescopes stretched over 100 feet (30 meters). They were so long, they could not be used easily. They could not be enclosed in tubes. Some were bare lenses attached to poles. They were controlled by ropes and pulleys.

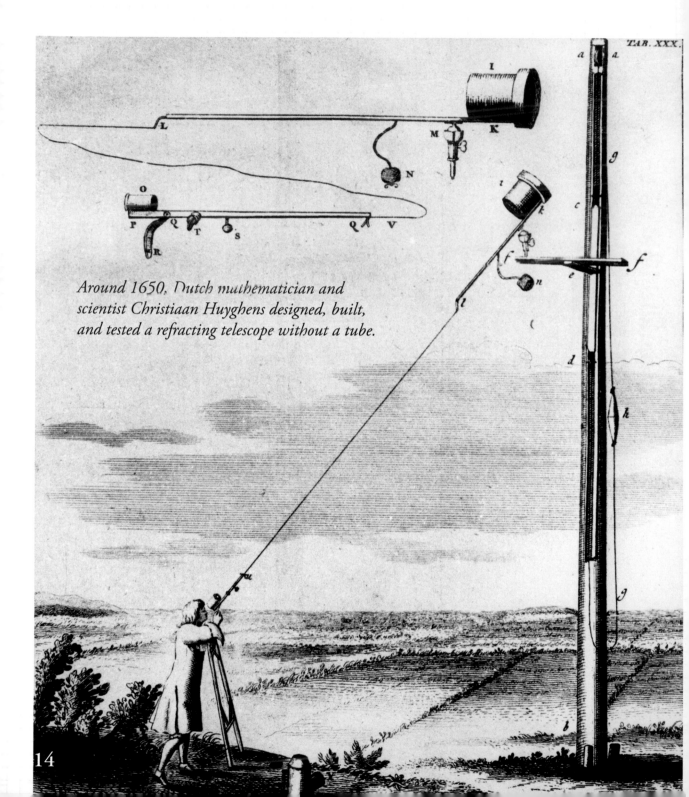

Around 1650, Dutch mathematician and scientist Christiaan Huyghens designed, built, and tested a refracting telescope without a tube.

In 1670, Polish astronomer Johannes Hevelius built a 150-foot (46-meter) telescope. It was so big, it was hung by ropes from a pole. Men on the ground moved it. The giant scope shook in the breeze. The ropes holding it constantly stretched and shrunk. Because it was so unsteady, the giant telescope was not used very often.

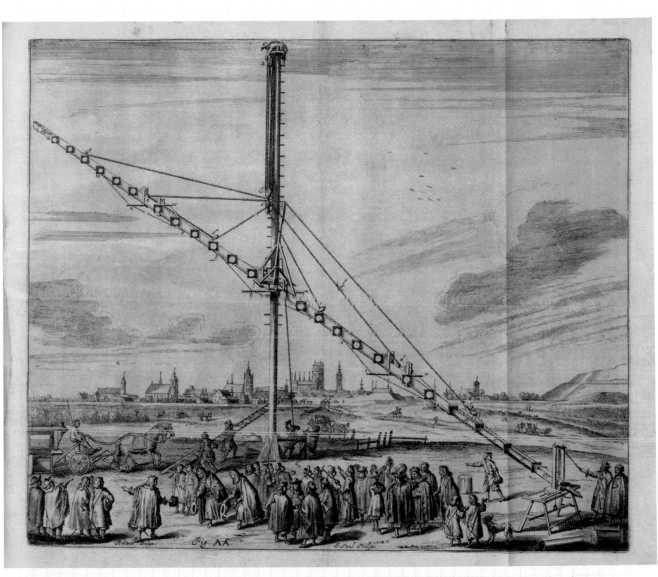

This 1673 illustration shows Polish astronomer Johannes Hevelius demonstrating his long refracting telescope while men on the ground pull on ropes to move the instrument.

Refracting telescopes have some disadvantages. They are often long and difficult to use because of their size. Also, the images from a refracting telescope can be blurry because of the way the lenses bend light.

World's Largest Refracting Telescope
The largest refracting telescope in the world is located at Yerkes Observatory in Williams Bay, Wisconsin. It was built in 1897. It features a 40-inch (102-centimeter) wide glass lens. Today, Yerkes uses the telescope in research and education programs.

1897 photo of the 40-inch (100-centimeter) refractor at the Yerkes Observatory.

2006 photo of the 40-inch (100-centimeter) refractor at the Yerkes Observatory.

Refracting telescopes also experience chromatic aberration. When visible light passes through a lens, it splits into its different colors. Each color focuses at a different point. This causes a fringe of color to appear around the image. Making the telescope's tube longer can reduce chromatic aberration.

A fringe of color appears around the edge of this image due to chromatic aberration, which can occur when a lens splits light rays into its different colors.

Reflecting Telescopes

In the 1660s, Sir Isaac Newton built a telescope using mirrors to focus light. This type of telescope is called a **reflecting** telescope. He replaced the telescope's lens with a spherical mirror. The mirror reflected and focused the light.

Sir Isaac Newton (1642–1726)

Using Mirrors
The larger a telescope's mirror, the more light it can collect. Telescopes work by collecting more light than the human eye can capture by itself. The more light the mirror collects, the better its image.

In Newton's telescope, light enters a tube at an open end. A convex primary mirror gathers light. It reflects it back to a focal point. Another mirror directs the light to an eyepiece on the side of the telescope. Newton found that using mirrors made the images much clearer.

Newton's first telescope

Newton's first telescope was only six inches (15.2 centimeters) long, but magnified objects almost 40 times. It achieved the same magnification as refracting telescopes that were three to six feet (0.9 to 1.8 meters) long.

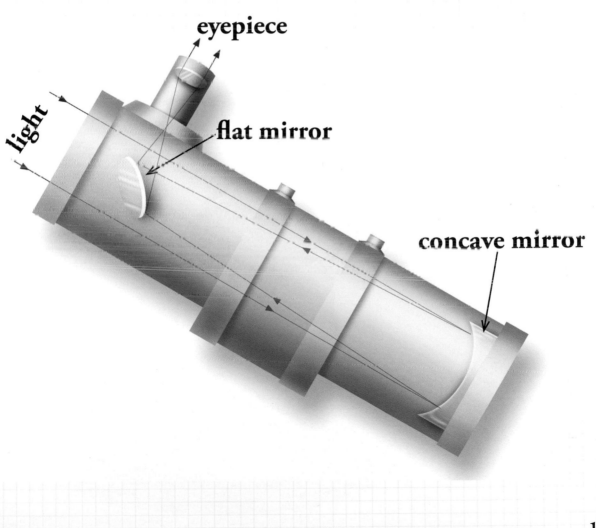

Reflecting telescopes are easier to use because they don't need large, heavy lenses. They are less expensive than refracting telescopes.

Reflecting telescopes can be built much larger than refracting telescopes. Reflecting telescopes use a mirror instead of a glass lens, so they do not produce chromatic aberration.

Newton solved the problem of chromatic aberration. Still, his telescope experienced another problem: spherical aberration. Parallel light rays that bounce off the edges of the spherical mirror focus closer than light rays that bounce off the center. Because there are many different focal points, the image is blurry. To see a clear image, all light rays must focus at the same point.

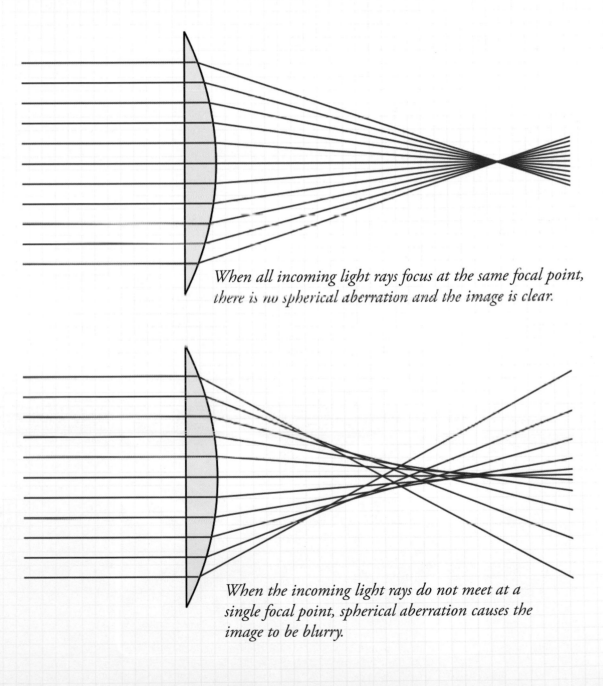

When all incoming light rays focus at the same focal point, there is no spherical aberration and the image is clear.

When the incoming light rays do not meet at a single focal point, spherical aberration causes the image to be blurry.

Large modern telescopes often use mirrors. Some have mirrors more than 33 feet (10 meters) in diameter. The largest reflecting telescope is the Gran Telescopio Canarias in Spain. It has a mirror diameter of 34.2 feet (10.4 meters).

European Extremely Large Telescope
Soon even larger reflecting telescopes will be in use. The European Extremely Large Telescope will have a primary mirror that is 129 feet (39.3 meters) in diameter. It is being built in Chile. Astronomers expect the telescope to be operating in the early 2020s.

Bigger and Better Telescopes

Technology and engineering advances over the centuries led to bigger and better telescopes. One of the most important developments was the parabolic mirror. A spherical mirror caused blurry images. So astronomers changed the mirror's shape to a **parabola**. They discovered it directed light rays to the same focal point. It produced clearer, sharper images.

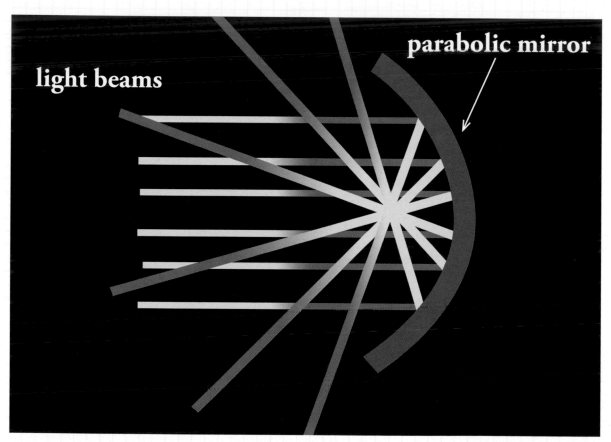

In this diagram, parallel beams of light strike a mirror shaped like a parabola. The parabolic mirror reflects the light beams to the same focal point.

In 1781, English astronomer William Herschel discovered the planet Uranus. He used a hand-built reflecting telescope. A few years later in 1789, Herschel built a 40-foot (12-meter) Newtonian reflector telescope. It was the first giant reflector telescope.

Leviathan of Parsonstown

In 1845, astronomer Lord Rosse built a reflecting telescope known as the "Leviathan of Parsonstown" at Birr Castle in Ireland. Using this telescope, Rosse was able to see the first spiral nebulae.

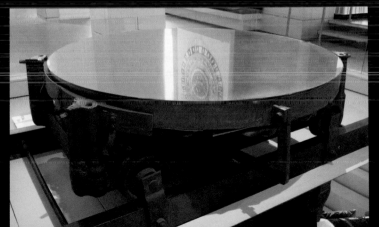

This original mirror with a six-foot (1.83-meter) diameter was used by Lord Rosse in his reflecting telescope.

Early reflecting telescopes used metal mirrors. These mirrors were made from tin and copper. Over time, these metal mirrors tarnished. They reflected less light.

In the 1850s, a German chemist named Justus Freiherr von Liebig used a chemical reaction to cover the surface of glass with a thin film of silver. The silver could be polished to create a mirror. Astronomers used this method to create telescope mirrors. This type of mirror was cheap, lightweight, and reflected more light than metal mirrors.

Justus Freiherr von Liebig (1803–1873)

◀ *This painting shows British astronomer William Herschel and his wife, Caroline, polishing a mirror to remove tarnish before it is used in a telescope.*

Astronomers used silver-coated glass mirrors instead of metal mirrors. They built even bigger and more powerful telescopes. In 1917, the 100-inch (2.54-meter) Hooker reflecting telescope opened at Mount Wilson Observatory in Pasadena, California.

With this telescope, astronomer Edwin Hubble discovered new galaxies. In 1924, he determined the distance to the Andromeda Nebula. He concluded the nebula lay far beyond the Milky Way galaxy.

Edwin Hubble (1889–1953)

American astronomer Edwin Hubble looks through the Hooker reflecting telescope for his research on new galaxies while at Mount Wilson Observatory.

Astronomers placed these large telescopes on high mountaintops, far away from city lights. There, the skies were darker. Some astronomers added cameras to their telescopes. A photograph revealed tiny stars and celestial objects that the eye could not see. Today's telescopes have cameras and other scientific instruments where the eyepiece used to be.

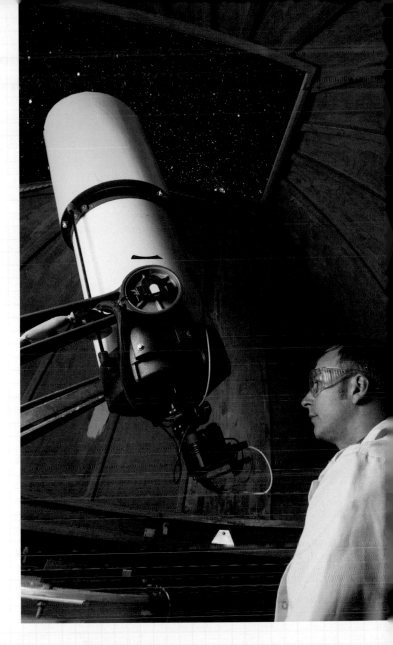

Discovery of Pluto

From the Lowell Observatory in Flagstaff, Arizona, Clyde Tombaugh discovered Pluto, the smallest and farthest planet in the Milky Way galaxy. Later, scientists reclassified Pluto as a dwarf planet. Unlike a regular planet, a dwarf planet does not have a clear path around the sun.

Hubble Space Telescope

Sometimes stars appear to twinkle. This happens when a star's light is distorted and bent by the Earth's **atmosphere**. As light passes through the atmosphere, it bends through warm and cool air pockets. Even the biggest, clearest telescopes on the ground experience the atmosphere's distortion.

To solve this problem, the National Aeronautics and Space Administration (NASA) and the European Space Agency designed a telescope to operate in space.

Astronomers used a space telescope to avoid the atmosphere's distortion. Launching a telescope into space is very complicated. It requires advanced instruments, computers, and spacecraft.

In April 1990, astronauts on the space shuttle *Discovery* deployed the Hubble Space Telescope. The telescope is a reflector with a 94.5-inch (2.4-meter) mirror. It orbits about 380 miles (600 kilometers) above Earth. It is equipped with instruments that give astronomers images of the universe. They can see visible, **infrared**, and ultraviolet light.

On April 24, 1990, the space shuttle Discovery *and its crew of five veteran astronauts launched from Earth. The mission carried the Hubble Space Telescope into space.*

Because it does not have distortion from Earth's atmosphere, the Hubble telescope gives astronomers more detailed looks at objects in space.

A Cassegrain Reflector

The Hubble is a Cassegrain reflector. Light hits its primary mirror and bounces to a secondary mirror. The second mirror focuses the light through a hole in the primary mirror and sends it to the telescope's scientific instruments.

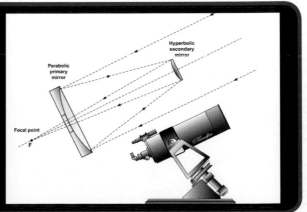

Hyperbolic secondary mirror

Parabolic primary mirror

Focal point
F

33

Every 97 minutes, the Hubble completes a trip around the Earth. As it moves, its mirrors capture light. They direct the light into instruments such as cameras, sensors, and spectrographs.

Solar Power
Sunlight powers the Hubble. The telescope has solar arrays that convert sunlight into electricity. Batteries store some electricity to power the telescope when it is in Earth's shadow.

The Hubble telescope has made more than 1.3 million observations. It takes pictures of the sun, stars, and planets as it orbits around Earth at about 17,000 miles (27,359 kilometers) per hour.

The reflecting telescope uses digital cameras to take pictures. Satellite communications send its images of space to astronomers on Earth.

Images Taken by the Hubble Telescope

Mars
April 2017

Jupiter
April 2017

Spiral in Andromeda
February 2017

Eagle Nebula
1995

Astronauts have visited Hubble several times. They repair broken parts. They replace old instruments with new ones. Each new instrument makes Hubble a more powerful space telescope. Using Hubble has helped astronomers further our understanding of the universe.

An astronaut works carefully to perform repairs and regular maintenance on the Hubble Space Telescope.

Space telescopes like Hubble have some drawbacks. They are expensive to build and launch. They cannot be as large as ground-based telescopes. And because they are in orbit, space telescopes are difficult to repair or upgrade.

National Aeronautics and Space Administration

STS-125

THE MISSION

Space shuttle Atlantis' STS-125 mission culminates the technological progress NASA has made to up-grade and enhance the Hubble Space Telescope's scientific capabilities. This is the 126th space shuttle mission, the 30th flight for Atlantis and the fifth and final shuttle Hubble servicing mission.

Two new instruments will be added to Hubble, the Cosmic Origins Spectrograph and the Wide Field Camera 3. A flight spare known as the Science Instrument Command and Data Handling system will replace one that failed on Hubble last year. The first in-orbit repairs will be made to the Space Telescope Imaging Spectrograph and the Advanced Camera for Surveys. The installation of new gyroscopes, battery modules and thermal blankets will support Hubble through at least 2014.

THE CREW

Commander Scott Altman will lead the crew and Gregory C. Johnson will serve as pilot. Mission specialists are veteran spacewalkers John Grunsfeld and Mike Massimino, as well as first-time space fliers Andrew Feustel, Michael Good and Megan McArthur.

www.nasa.gov

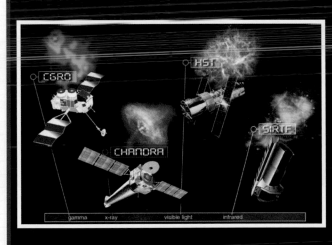

NASA's Great Observatories
NASA built four orbiting telescopes known as the Great Observatories— the Hubble Space Telescope, the Chandra X-Ray Observatory, the Compton Gamma Ray Observatory, and the Spitzer Space Telescope. These telescopes give NASA a picture of objects in space across different wavelengths of light. All except the Compton are still in orbit.

A New Generation of Telescopes

The first telescopes only used visible light. Modern, sophisticated telescopes allow astronomers to see other types of light and radiation in space. They use radio waves, microwaves, infrared, ultraviolet, x-rays, and gamma rays. Using these telescopes, astronomers can see new details in space.

NASA's Spitzer Space Telescope detects infrared light and allows scientists to see areas in space hidden from optical telescopes, such as the centers of galaxies and newly forming planetary systems.

Many objects in space produce radio-frequency radiation. In 1931, American engineer Karl Jansky was the first person to detect radio radiation in space. He discovered radio waves coming from the center of the Milky Way galaxy. His discovery inspired the new field of radio astronomy.

Karl Jansky (1905–1950)

Radio telescopes use a large parabolic dish to collect radio waves. The radio waves bounce off the dish. They meet at a single focal point. A receiver captures and amplifies the radio waves. It sends them to a computer. Using radio telescopes, astronomers study the frequency, power, and timing of radio waves from celestial objects.

Chandra is the world's most powerful x-ray telescope. Scientists use Chandra for many missions, including studying black holes and analyzing comets in the solar system.

Using infrared telescopes, astronomers view objects that are invisible to optical telescopes. They study interstellar gas, dust discs around other stars, and failed stars (brown dwarfs) with infrared light. Other telescopes allow astronomers to see high energy X and gamma rays. Each type of telescope helps astronomers learn more about space.

NASA is also building another space telescope, the James Webb Space Telescope. This telescope will be bigger than the Hubble. Unlike the Hubble, it will not orbit Earth. Instead, it will orbit the sun.

Webb's Primary Mirror
The Webb's primary mirror is made of 18 separate segments. The mirror will unfold and adjust its shape after launch. Its primary mirror will be able to gather 10 times the amount of light the Hubble can gather.

Scientists direct the placement of 18 flight mirror segments that make up the primary mirror on NASA's James Webb Space Telescope.

The Webb Telescope is an infrared telescope. It will make observations in infrared light. The Webb will help astronomers see even more of the universe. They hope to learn more about how stars and planets are formed and how galaxies evolve.

The James Webb Space Telescope is scheduled to launch in 2018. It will be used by thousands of astronomers worldwide.

With computers, astronomers are able to design new, powerful telescopes. Multi-mirror telescopes use multiple mirrors. The mirrors work together. They are easier to control and operate than one huge mirror. They still have the same light-collecting power. Computers control the shape and position of each mirror.

At NASA's Goddard Space Flight Center in Maryland, the Flight Operations Team monitors data being sent to Earth from the Hubble Space Telescope.

Computers also made another technology possible. Adaptive optics reduces the atmosphere's distortion in ground telescopes. A computer controls the shape of the telescope's mirror. It reads distortions in the atmosphere. Then it constantly changes the mirror's shape to keep light rays aimed at one focal point. This creates the clearest images ever seen from ground telescopes.

Telescopes are engineering wonders. And as technology improves, so will their design. What discoveries do you think future telescopes might bring? It's exciting to consider!

The Keck-2 telescope projects a sodium laser that allows scientists to explore the sky with adaptive optics and reduce the atmosphere's distortion and blurring of incoming light.

Glossary

astronomer (us-STRON-uh-mer): a person who studies stars, planets, and space

atmosphere (AT-muhss-fihr): the mixture of gases that surrounds a planet

celestial (suh-LES-chuhl): to do with the sky or the heavens

convex (KON-veks): curved outward, like the outer side of a ball

focal point (FOH-kuhl POINT): the point where rays of light meet after being bent by a lens

infrared (in-FRUH-red): producing or using rays of light that cannot be seen with the naked eye and are longer than the rays produced by red light

lenses (LENZ-es): pieces of curved glass that bend light

optical (OP-tuh-kuhl): designed to aid sight

parabola (puh-RAB-uh-luh): a special curve shaped like an arch

reflecting (ri-FLEKT-ing): to bounce rays of light off an object such as a mirror

refracting (ri-FRACKT-ing): changing direction when traveling from one medium to another

Index

Show What You Know

1. How does a refracting telescope work?
2. How does a reflecting telescope work?
3. What are the advantages of a reflecting telescope?
4. How does Earth's atmosphere affect images seen through a telescope?
5. Why does focal point affect a telescope's length?

Websites to Visit

www.ngm.nationalgeographic.com/2009/07/telescopes/telescopes-interactive

www.nasa.gov/audience/forstudents/9-12/features/telescope_feature_912.html

http://spaceplace.nasa.gov/telescope-mirrors/en

About the Author

Carla Mooney has written many books for children and young adults. She lives in Pennsylvania with her husband and three children. She enjoys learning about how things work in the world around her.

Meet The Author!
www.meetREMauthors.com

www.rourkeeducationalmedia.com

PHOTO CREDITS: Cover and title page: ©Triff; table of contents, p.40: ©PhonlamaiPhoto; p.4-5: ©Christopher Badzioch; p.6: ©ilbusca; p.7: ©nicoolay; p.7, 12, 15, 18, 21, 33, 39: Wiki; p.8, 32, 33, 35, 36, 38, 41, 42, 43, 44: Courtesy of NASA; p.8: ©TonyBaggett; p.10: ©Master3D; p.14, 19: ©World History Archive/Alamy Stock Photo; p.17: ©S953554; p.18: ©Floortje; p.19: ©BSIP SA/Alamy Stock Photo; p.20: ©Alexandr Mitiuc; p.22-23: ©holbox; p.22: ©Astrofireball | Dreamstime.com; p.26: ©Wellcome Library, London. Wellcome Images; p.28: ©Pictorial Press Ltd/Alamy Stock Photo; p.29: ©Stolk, ©Nostalgia for Infinity; p.30-31: ©ClaudioVentrella; p.34: ©jamesbenet; p.39: ©Neutronman; p.45: ©Richard Wainscoat/Alamy Stock Photo

Edited by: Keli Sipperley
Cover and interior design by: Rhea Magaro-Wallace

Library of Congress PCN Data

Telescopes / Carla Mooney
(Engineering Wonders)
ISBN 978-1-68342-390-4 (hard cover)(alk.paper)
ISBN 978-1-68342-460-4 (soft cover)
ISBN 978-1-68342-556-4 (e-Book)
Library of Congress Control Number: 2017931282

Rourke Educational Media
Printed in the United States of America, North Mankato, Minnesota

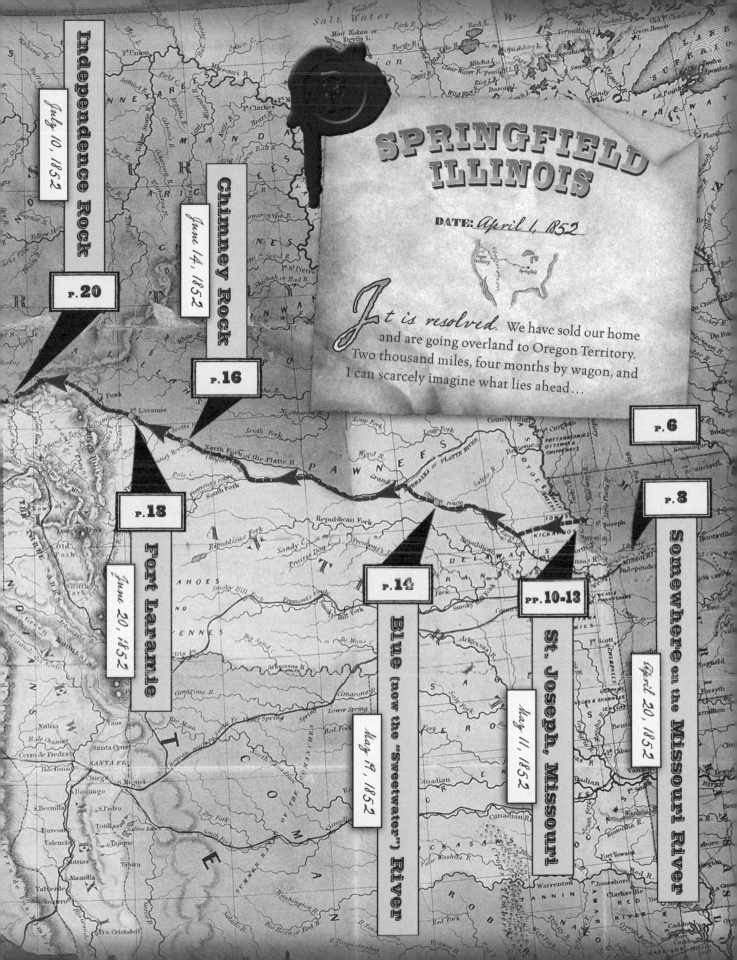

SPRINGFIELD ILLINOIS

DATE: *April 1, 1852*

It is resolved. We have sold our home and are going overland to Oregon Territory. Two thousand miles, four months by wagon, and I can scarcely imagine what lies ahead...

P. 6

Independence Rock
July 10, 1852
P.20

Chimney Rock
June 14, 1852
P.16

Fort Laramie
June 20, 1852
P.18

P. 8

Somewhere on the Missouri River
April 20, 1852

P.14

Blue (now the "Sweetwater") River
May 19, 1852

PP.10-13

St. Joseph, Missouri
May 11, 1852

SPRINGFIELD ILLINOIS

DATE: *April 1, 1852*

Abraham Lincoln served our state government as a congressman here. I consider him my friend, as my father treated him once for melancholia.

It is resolved. We have sold our home and are going overland to Oregon Territory. Two thousand miles, four months by wagon, and I can scarcely imagine what lies ahead. Father cannot contain his excitement. "In coin, we are neither rich nor poor, but live in relative comfort," he told us all at supper last night, conducting an imaginary orchestra with his knife. "But it is not in our nature to be content with comfort. Your great-grandfather crossed the broad ocean from Scotland to Massachusetts to find fields expansive enough for his dreams. Your grandfather journeyed from Massachusetts to Illinois to educate the youth of our new frontier. Your forebears followed the siren call of opportunity ever westward, and now our time has come. Oregon brims with unclaimed land, with emigrants hopeful for the future and needful of our services. And so we set out into the wilderness, knowing not from whence our next meal will come…" I remember little after that but the anxious clatter of forks as we sought to fill ourselves with nourishment before preparing to set off into the land of opportunity.

MY PRIVATE FEARS

I am excited, for every writer needs inspiration, and more than a few have gotten it miles from home. But I am scared, and I do not mind confessing my fears for our journey.

- ☞ **Starvation** (I am fond of eating and do not wish to give it up)

- ☞ **Thirst** (we will be crossing the Great American Desert)

- ☞ **Death** by drowning (how is it that we must ford rivers by the score in order to cross the desert?)

- ☞ **Indians** (the skin atop my head has served me well these 15 years, keeping the sun off my brain and all that)

My family and traveling companions

As a journalist, I have interviewed each of them about their hopes and dreams for our new life in the West.

My elder brother, Nathan Reed
TRADE: **APPRENTICE BLACKSMITH**

"Why, to make my fortune. In Oregon, a blacksmith is worth the weight of his anvil in gold."

My mother, Eliza Reed
TRADE: **MANAGER OF JOHN REED**

"My hope is that your father's dreams do not make us paupers."

My elder sister, Abigail Reed
TRADE: **QUEEN OF FAMILY**

"I speak only to real journalists."

My father, John Reed
TRADE: **PHYSICIAN**

(I have more than adequately recorded his thoughts.)

My grandfather, Silas Reed
TRADE: **SCHOOLMASTER**

"I'm sorry, Will, but my traveling days are done."

Me, William Reed
TRADE: **WRITER**

As for me, I append this letter from the editor of our newspaper here in Springfield.

Dear Mr. William Reed,

I would be pleased to receive your letters from the trail and to consider them for publication. Our readers are eager for news from the West.

Sincerely,
Mr. Allen Francis
Illinois State Journal

SOMEWHERE
ON THE
MISSOURI RIVER

DATE: *April 20, 1852*

This is James Marsden and "his" negro, Joseph. Though the slave state, Missouri, is our neighbor, I have never before seen a man who has been bought and sold like a head of cattle.

The day may come when I stand on solid ground, but I do not know when. We were a week on the road to St. Louis in a coach that still contains three of my teeth, rattled by turns out of my head. We now sway and lurch aboard a steamboat so large it suggests they have discovered how to make a city float (like the one I am pasting in here). On the upper deck, there are 700 tons of wagons, pig (dead and smoked), cattle (alive, to judge from the smell), and more. All of it is bound for the West. Have not yet seen an Indian, but it is said that they are set to trade places with us and move east. They have seen so many people going the other way that they wonder how there can be any white people left in the States. We are to travel in company with others for mutual aid and protection. My father has enlisted fellow travelers on the boat. I have sketched here three of his more questionable choices.

This preening fellow is called Byron Strong. I don't care for him, but Abigail does. She will have to beware his father, Ezra, who is a preacher. If God is as stern as he is, we are all in trouble.

Mother says that in my journal I am to keep a record of our transactions along the way for she does not want to go broke getting to the land of opportunity.

I am told that our steamboat cost $50,000 to make but that the owner will make it back in a single season.

LEDGER

DATE:	April 1-20
BEGINNING BALANCE:	
Savings, sale of house:	$1,850.00
INCOME:	$0
EXPENSES:	
Stagecoach, Springfield to St. Louis ($8/passenger):	$40.00
Meals:	$75.00
Steamboat, St. Louis to St. Joe ($12/passenger & $12 freight):	• $72.00
CURRENT BALANCE:	$1,663.00

BEN CAMPBELL

This man calls himself *Stannard*. He says he has a nose for gold and struck it rich on the stuff in California. He is bound for Green River, where he opened a trading post with his profits.

St. Joseph, Missouri
April 28, 1852

Here is the last outpost of civilization, where the entire population of the United States is outfitting itself before setting off for the West.

Our company now numbers 66 people and 14 wagons.

We met a man who is set on driving 2,000 turkeys to Oregon. He bought them at 50 cents a head and says he will sell them for $8 when he arrives.

MISSOURI MILLS

Grist mills turn out flour by the ton for the emigrants. I aim to be sure we have enough for pie.

We saw several "Bloomer costumes." Nathan wondered if they have invented a third sex, between male and female. For his wit he received a blow to the head from Abigail.

Blacksmiths like this one make last-minute repairs to a battalion of wagons. Nathan claims we could make our fortune on the trail if we were not in such a hurry to get to Oregon.

I have survived my first encounter with the Indians, who mingle in the streets without anyone marking it strange. Some have rifles and are dressed no differently from a white man.

Stannard prowls the town, crowing about his knowledge of the West. He sells maps— "only" $50—to a lake in California that is supposedly full of gold.

ST. JOSEPH MISSOURI

DATE: *May 11, 1852*

Our Purchases

4 yoke oxen	$280.00
(I have named them Lincoln, Clay, Garrison, Washington, Jefferson, Adams, Cooper, & Irving.)	
2 Milk cows	80.00
1 Donkey	50.00
1 Wagon	150.00
3 Rifles	60.00
Lead, 30 lbs.	1.50
Powder, 25 lbs.	5.50
Flour, 1,000 lbs.	150.00
Bacon, 450 lbs.	60.00
Coffee, 25 lbs.	12.50
Tea, 5 lbs.	2.75
Sugar, 125 lbs.	67.50
Pickles, one barrel, 20 lbs.	10.00
Dried fruit, 50 lbs.	3.00
Salt, pepper, &c., 50 lbs.	3.00
Lard, 50 lbs.	2.50
Saleratus, 10 lbs	1.00
Cooking utensils, 30 lbs.	4.00
Tent, 30 lbs	5.00
Bedding, 45 lbs.	22.50
Matches	1.00
Candles and soap	7.00
Clothes, tools, etc., 230 lbs.	0
(brought from home)	
Total ..... 2,175 lbs.	**$978.75**

"How much for saleratus!?" "Why did you spend so dearly on the bacon? I could have had it for 20 cents to the pound." "An entire barrel of pickles!? Dear, we will sink into the plains."

Mother's preachings have nearly made me long for Father's speeches, but he has been silenced by the strain of preparations. I think that Mother secretly believes that we are foolish to trade a decent life for something completely unknown. But she is a practical person and once committed to a course of action, wants to see it through in the best way possible. She is eager to leave St. Joe, and so am I. The merchants here sell their goods at one price to local residents and reserve their highest prices for the emigrants. Our trail guidebook (30 cents) tells us that the smart traveler will be on the plains by May 1 or risk being trapped in the early snows at the western mountains. Still, we cannot leave. The Indians say that the prairie grasses are late this year and our cattle will have nothing to eat. So we wait. Mother has spent four days now checking her list with our pile of supplies.

I saw an amazing contraption very much like this one as we passed Independence, 20 miles downriver. It was invented by a man called Wind-Wagon Thomas, who claims he can make 15 miles per hour across the prairie with a good breeze.

Our Chariot

We store valuables here for safekeeping.

False floor. We store provisions beneath it and sleep on top, though I think I will prefer to sleep under the stars.

Rub the wagon bed with tar and it will float— or, so they claim.

Wheels must be greased daily with lard from a buffalo or other unfortunate creature.

This is called the "tongue." Mother has given strict orders to stay clear of it while we are moving.

Rope, water, grease buckets, spare spokes, and my sister (if necessary) will be stored here.

Mr. Ox for President?

There is so much impassioned debate here over which animal is best suited to pull us to Oregon that one would think we are debating the future leadership of our country. And so, I ask, who is to be the next president of these United States: Mr. Ox, Mr. Mule, or Mr. Horse?

	FOR	AGAINST
OX	✸ Strong ✸ Durable ✸ Dumb enough to pull 2,500 pounds across a continent without protest ✸ Considers prairie grass a delicacy	✸ Spooks easily ✸ Tends to stampede for water
MULE	✸ Fast ✸ Enjoys cottonwood bark when grass is not on the menu	✸ Stubborn and brutish ✸ Not as strong as Mr. Ox
HORSE	✸ Very fast	✸ Often stolen by Sioux or other Indians ✸ Not very strong ✸ Not durable

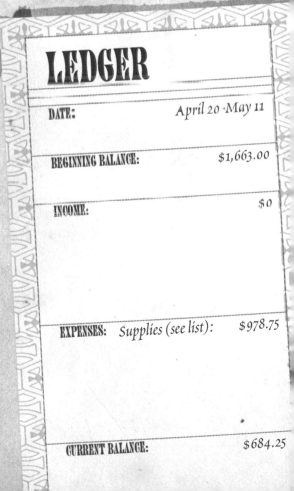

LEDGER

DATE:	April 20 –May 11
BEGINNING BALANCE:	$1,663.00
INCOME:	$0
EXPENSES: Supplies (see list):	$978.75
CURRENT BALANCE:	$684.25

BLUE (NOW THE "SWEETWATER") RIVER

DATE: May 19, 1852

We are on the trail at last, yet Mother is not happy. The churning rivers have got us already, and she must make a new list. Here is how it happened: Seven days out from St. Joseph, we reached the Big Blue. The water was low, and many in our company wanted to ford as we could easily walk the oxen across. Father felt it safer to take the ferry and negotiated a fair price of $1.50 a wagon. We camped the night, and when we woke, rain had come and swelled the river. Seeing that we could not cross by ourselves if we wanted to, the ferryman raised his price to $3. Father was willing to pay it, but "Mr. Master" (Mr. Marsden) refused and had a scrap with the ferryman, whereby several men appeared with rifles to emphasize the fairness of the fee. After much debate, it was decided to move on and find a place to ford. And that was our error. Halfway across, Lincoln lost his footing, and the rest of the team went with him. We lost half our flour to the river and all our sugar. Our guidebook tells us the Sweetwater River is still 500 miles distant, but given the way we have sweetened this river, I have borrowed its name for the Big Blue.

We have passed 14 new made graves, and father is worried for us. He has already treated several people for the measles and for cholera.

Poles (like the one this boatman wields) are important at river crossings—if used wisely. It was Nathan's job to cross first, test for quicksand, and plant poles where the ground was SUPPOSEDLY firm.

From my friend J. Goldsborough Bruff,

who preceded me on the trail by three years. He chose the gold fields over Oregon, but returned home rich only in memories, which he committed to paper with an expert eye.

Taken from the E. bank

Here are the two other choices for *river crossings*, neither of them good. Ferries are often makeshift rafts made of logs, canoes, or wagon beds lashed together. Most bridges are as perilous as the one Bruff drew here. Some are run by Indians. The Sac and Fox, for example, have a bridge at Wolf Creek. We paid them $1 a wagon and 25 cents an animal to cross.

Perilous ferriage of the Missouri, 7 miles below old Ft. Kearny. — June 1, 2, 3, & 4th 1849 (during a great freshet)

above St. Joseph's

Nathan insists we would earn more than $5,000 if we settled for the summer and built our own bridge. His plea seemed to interest Mother, but Father would hear nothing of it.

Bruff May 23d 1849

CHIMNEY ROCK

DATE: June 14, 1852

A wonder of nature: Standing beside Chimney Rock, we felt no bigger than insects.

The cholera has us in its grip, and the Platte River is littered with broken dreams. Still we press on, the entire population of the country rolling through the dust to its grave. It is a terrible disease, and I have intimate knowledge of it, as I have been helping Father treat patients up and down the trail. It begins with diarrhea, then turns to cramps in the stomach and legs, and finally to vomiting. It results in death for half the people we treat. Father does not know what causes it but says its victims seem to have drunk bad water or breathed noxious air. Mr. Strong is more certain. He says it is God's vengeance for our sins, though I do not understand why God would have chosen the five-year-old girl with the blonde plaits who died yesterday. She could not yet have done anything to warrant such a punishment. Her family tore boards from their wagon to build her a proper coffin.

Cholera Morbus

is about as sure to come as Summer is. It comes suddenly and without warning — is Dangerous and often Fatal.

ARE YOU PREPARED

for its coming?

If any of your family are attacked "PROMPT action only may save life. For 46 YEARS ONE medicine has ALWAYS cured CHOLERA, CHOLERA MORBUS, DIARRHOEA, DYSENTERY and all SUMMER COMPLAINTS. CHILDREN can take it with perfect safety.

This medicine is

Perry Davis' Pain Killer.

To be on the safe side get some NOW and have it on hand. For sale by all Druggists.

PERRY DAVIS & SON, Props. PROVIDENCE, R.I.

Father says popular remedies such as this are "humbuggery," He gives calomel, laudanum, and mint tea for cholera, but his scientific treatments do not seem to gain better results.

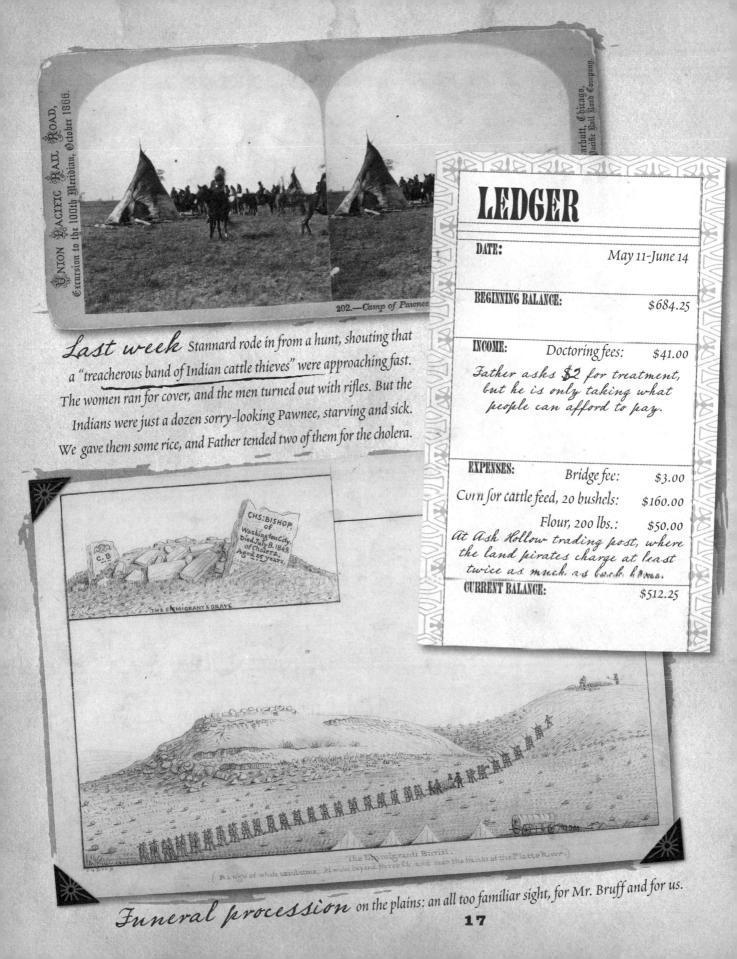

UNION PACIFIC RAIL ROAD, Excursion to the 100th Meridian, October 1866.

Harbutt, Chicago, Pacific Rail Road Company.

202.—Camp of Pawnee

Last week Stannard rode in from a hunt, shouting that a "treacherous band of Indian cattle thieves" were approaching fast. The women ran for cover, and the men turned out with rifles. But the Indians were just a dozen sorry-looking Pawnee, starving and sick. We gave them some rice, and Father tended two of them for the cholera.

CHS: BISHOP of Washington City, Died July 8, 1849, of cholera; Aged 25 years.

C. B.

THE EMIGRANT'S GRAVE.

LEDGER

DATE:	May 11–June 14

BEGINNING BALANCE:	$684.25

INCOME:	Doctoring fees:	$41.00

Father asks $2 for treatment, but he is only taking what people can afford to pay.

EXPENSES:	Bridge fee:	$3.00
	Corn for cattle feed, 20 bushels:	$160.00
	Flour, 200 lbs.:	$50.00

At Ash Hollow trading post, where the land pirates charge at least twice as much as back home.

CURRENT BALANCE:	$512.25

The Emigrant's Burial.
(Range of white sandstone, 9 miles beyond Horse Ck. and near the banks of the Platte River.)

Funeral procession on the plains: an all too familiar sight, for Mr. Bruff and for us.

FORT LARAMIE

DATE: *June 20, 1852*

t *Fort Laramie* we camped for two days and barely saw Nathan all the while. He disappeared into the ramshackle huts of the traders that have bought themselves Indian brides from the local chieftains and settled around the fort. Most of the traders are mountain men who used to trap for fur in the Rockies. When beaver fur went out of fashion in Europe, they decided to trap desperate emigrants instead and charge them a fortune for supplies. That doesn't trouble Nathan's conscience in the least. Once again he is filling our ears full of numbers. He claims that chewing tobacco bought for 20 cents a pound in Santa Fe can be sold for $1 on the trail and $5 in Salt Lake City. Father is straining to keep him on the trail with us. We traded two rifles for some buffalo hides, as we are nearing the mountains, where it gets cold at night.

A Sioux brave offered to buy Abigail for ten fine horses. My father politely told him that white people do not sell women. The Sioux gestured to the traders and wondered why not, when at least some white men are willing to buy Indian brides.

The sutler here has luxuries we have not seen for many dusty miles. Abigail talked father into buying a jar of lemon syrup for $1.25. I purchased a 10-cent bottle of ink for 30 cents.

18

LEDGER

DATE: June 14-20

BEGINNING BALANCE: $512.25

INCOME: $0

EXPENSES:

1 Jar lemon syrup:	$1.25
Ink:	$.30
5 Buffalo hides:	2 rifles

Barter is just as good as cash on the trail.

CURRENT BALANCE: $510.70

Abigail has left her dresses in a heap and joined the third sex, leaving Mr. Strong to pray furiously she does not bring the cholera back. Byron is even more smitten than before.

The fort was the scene, last September, of a great tribal council. Indian chiefs from the Arapahos, Cheyennes, Sioux, Assiniboins, Snakes, Arikaras, Gros Ventres, and Crows agreed to keep peace on the trail and allow emigrants through unmolested. In exchange, the government agreed to give them $50,000 in goods every year.

INDEPENDENCE ROCK

DATE: *July 10, 1852*

We have finally left the Platte and the dread cholera behind. Yet each day yields plenty more to trouble us. Travel has been steep as we approach the mountains. A stubble of sagebrush covers the trail. There is grass here, but it is the first we have seen for miles, and the animals have eaten the corn we bought at Ash Hollow. Good drinking water is scarce. We still pass no fewer than five graves each day, and now we must add to it the stench of dead and dying cattle.

But all talk here is of the Sioux, who are said to be out for revenge. We are told that a party of braves took over a ferry outside Laramie, claiming it was rightfully theirs. A detachment of soldiers took it back, and one of the braves fired a shot before fleeing. The soldiers tracked down the Sioux and killed three of them. Byron tells me we have left Sioux territory and are in the domain of the Crow, but still we fear for our safety and for our cattle. At night we circle the wagons for protection.

A VIEW from
exhibiting the S

Father addressed us all on this very spot, urging us not to lose hope. "Nature has laid before you a stern test. Endure it and she will present you with all the fruits of a land unscarred by frost or drought."

We climbed Independence Rock and wrote our names in axle grease alongside a thousand others. Byron and Abigail wrote theirs together.

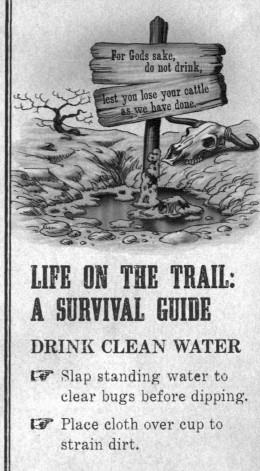

For Gods sake, do not drink, lest you lose your cattle as we have done.

LIFE ON THE TRAIL: A SURVIVAL GUIDE

DRINK CLEAN WATER

☞ Slap standing water to clear bugs before dipping.

☞ Place cloth over cup to strain dirt.

CLEAN LICE FROM CLOTHES

☞ Place over anthill to make a feast for the ants.

AVOID HAZARDS

☞ Read everything you see; your fellow travelers mean to be helpful.

When cattle die of starvation, we are eager to take what meat we can so we do not meet the same fate.

Skinning a Buffalo

South Pass

July 15, 1852

We are encamped on the central ridge of the continent. Here are the first waters we have seen that flow to the West. Tomorrow we will follow them.

Father gathered his strength for some speechifying tonight. "We stand here at the summit of our lives, the past laid out to our east, the future to our west..." and so on.

I have sent several entries from my journal east with a mail wagon for 50 cents, though I am not optimistic they will ever arrive.

It is powerful cold here tonight and the peaks around us are painted with snow. I found Joseph chained to a wagon as Mr. Master fears he will run off. I offered him my buffalo hide, but he would not take it.

Mr. Strong and Father argued for some time tonight, and I found Abigail mad as a wet hen. It seems Mr. Strong says he will have no one "dressed in the devil's garments" shining up to his son. He is breaking with the company and moving ahead tomorrow.

We have circled the wagons each night to pen the cattle and allow the sentries to guard more effectively against the Sioux.

Stannard and his cronymen have refused guard duty since we left St. Joe. They prefer to gamble at cards, and they have found no shortage of makeshift games along the way.

LITTLE COLORADO DESERT

DATE: *July 20, 1852*

The oxen are gone, and we are in despair, thanks to a band of hostile Sioux. My brother saw it happen, but neither he nor anyone else could prevent it. Nathan and three other men from our company had driven the animals six miles off trail to find tolerably good grass for them to eat. As they were taking their noontime meal with the beasts, several young Indian braves rode headlong for the herd whooping and firing rifles in the air. The animals spooked and left their dining place at a full run. Nathan and the others ran for their horses, only to find that they too had been stolen. They could do nothing but watch as the oxen, our faithful guides to the West, disappeared into a cloud of dust toward the Green River.

Here is the toll taken by the Indian for our passage through his hunting ground.

Nathan rode a borrowed horse ahead to Green River, at Stannard's urging. Stannard's associates there have an abundance of cattle to sell, though the beasts are miserable specimens.

Nathan spent our last savings on four yoke of oxen and returned with a plan that I will reveal shortly.

Mother allowed herself to wonder aloud why we left comfortable circumstances in Springfield for this. But she gathered herself to press ahead. My family combined with another, which had no oxen to pull their wagon. Each family left half their belongings in a heap by the trail and set off in a single wagon.

Father, Mother, and Abigail will move on to Fort Hall while Nathan and I stay behind and attempt to rebuild our savings.

LEDGER	
DATE:	June 20–July 20
BEGINNING BALANCE:	$510.70
INCOME:	$0
EXPENSES: 4 Yoke oxen:	$500.00
CURRENT BALANCE:	$10.70

Green River Ferry

July 28, 1852

Here is Nathan's plan: The Reed Brothers Ferry.

The crossing is hazardous, and rumor has it that 40 souls lie buried in the banks downstream. This boy, who saved a yoke of oxen, was more fortunate. He lost only his pants and socks to the current.

We use the beds of two old wagons, lashed together and sealed with tar. We have hired a pilot to guide the ferry by rope and another to pole.

Stannard has stayed behind with the traders here. Some say these men burn grassland so emigrants will be obliged to sell their starving cattle cheap. The traders turn around and sell them to people like my mother and father, who in their desperation will pay any price.

Thomas Moor holds a charter from the Mormons, who claim the right to license ferry operators in these parts. We have set up downriver from Moor and are charging half the price.

FERRY ↑

Nathan earns extra money fixing wagon wheels after the ferry stops for the evening. I may have to bind him to a horse to get him away from this place.

REED FERRY $6

LEDGER

DATE:	July 20-27
BEGINNING BALANCE:	$10.70

INCOME:

Ferry (135 wagons at $6 ea.):	$810.00
Ferry (320 animals at $.25 ea.):	$80.00
Blacksmithing:	$262.00

EXPENSES:

2 Ferry operators (5 days at $15/day ea.):	$150.00
Food and supplies:	$52.00

CURRENT BALANCE:	$960.70

GREEN RIVER

DATE: *July 28, 1852*

Nathan and I paid a visit to the trading post yesterday and discovered a suspicious sight: a healthy ox that bore a strong resemblance to Garrison. We investigated further, and I believe we have solved the mystery of our missing cattle and unmasked the "Indian" thieves. Here are the clues:

* An "R" branded onto another ox that looked suspiciously like Irving.

* An Indian costume of buffalo hide and feathers, found on a noontime visit to Stannard's tent.

* A horse looking much like Nathan's, corralled with a dozen more behind the trading post.

The "Indians" who stampeded our livestock were none other than Stannard and his cronies, dressed for a costume ball. We are not sure what to do, as the traders are a rough lot and well armed. In the meantime, we had the Mormons to vex us.

We are in Utah Territory now, and it is run by the Mormons like a country. They maintain their own army, called the Nauvoo Legion.

This stern fellow is Brigham Young, the leader of the Mormons. He has led his followers west by the thousands to find a home where they can worship in peace. He told them to settle in a place no one else wanted, and so they built their capital, Salt Lake City, in a desert where the only water is spoiled by salt. The Mormons seem to be making the best of it. They do not own the trading post at Green River, but they have taken over ferry operations along this part of the trail. Like all the ferry operators from Kansas on out, they do not take kindly to competition, and we are not sure how long they will let us operate.

BRANLEY PASS

DATE: *August 7, 1852*

After riding hard for a day, we are bound for Fort Hall with cattle in tow, and here is how it happened. We decided not to anger the Mormons any longer but to take our revenge against the traders and be done with Green River. We packed our meager belongings and our earnings, leaving Nathan's smithy tools behind. Under cover of darkness, we stole back Nathan's horse and one other. We rode first to the east and left a message on the trail to warn unsuspecting emigrants of the scoundrels at Green River. Passing back through, we engaged in some trickery of our own, setting a dozen horses and a hundred head of cattle free to move on to Oregon or wherever they choose. By first light we were well along our way, driving Garrison, Irving, and six new oxen toward a reunion with our family.

EAST

BEWARE

WEST

LEDGER

DATE: July 27–Aug. 7

BEGINNING BALANCE: $960.70

INCOME:

Ferry (262 wagons at $6 ea.): $1,668.00

Ferry (828 animals at $.25 ea.): $207.00

Blacksmithing: $495.00

EXPENSES:

2 Ferry operators
(10 days at $15/day ea.): $300.00

Food and supplies: $60.00

CURRENT BALANCE: $2,970.70

Land or Lucre?

Flush with coin from our ferry operation, Nathan says he wants to take the California Trail after Fort Hall and try to strike it rich in the gold fields. He says California is the place where men make real fortunes; in Oregon they merely toil their lives away in obscurity. We debated by the fire, and here, as I see it, are the arguments for both.

	FOR	AGAINST
CALIFORNIA 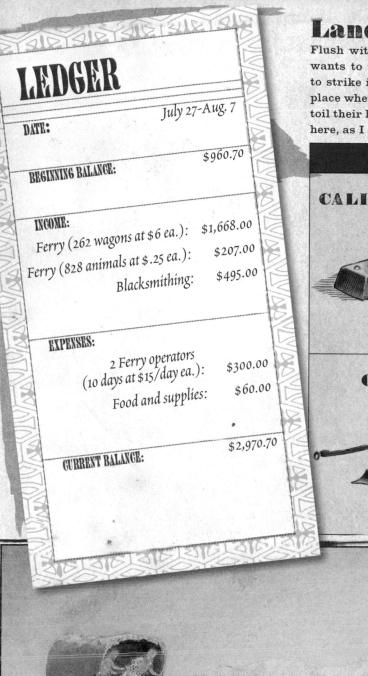	✳ Adventure ✳ Miners can earn $30 a day	✳ Less than 1 in 12 residents are women ✳ Miners can spend $35 a day to keep themselves fed and clothed ✳ Backbreaking labor
OREGON	✳ Government gives 160 acres to single men, 320 to married couples ✳ Fewer scoundrels such as Stannard	✳ Fewer opportunities to find wealth quickly

BEWARE THE WATER: A SURVIVAL GUIDE

☞ Many of the streams in these parts are poisoned with alkali, yet the cattle are so desperate we cannot keep them from drinking.

☞ Signs of alkali poisoning: swelling on stomach and chest, cough, death.

☞ Cure: Pour grease or water mixed with flour down the animal's throat.

FORT HALL

DATE: *August 12, 1852*

Oregon Spectator.

OREGON CITY:

TUESDAY, JULY

We arrived Fort Hall after a six-day journey driving the oxen from Green River. Father and Mother and Abigail were much relieved to see us. I thought that I noticed a tear even in Abigail's eye, but she composed herself quickly and informed us that accomodations at Fort Hall were inferior and we should have come earlier.

The reunion did not last long before we turned to more practical matters. We purchased a new wagon and gave the one we were sharing, including the old oxen, to the family Mother and Father had combined with. And so, we press on.

A man coming east had a supply of newspapers from Oregon City. We purchased one for 50 cents. I asked the man if he would consider my journal for publication. He laughed and said I would have to wait and ask the editor when we arrived.

Four days' ride

from Fort Hall, we came across a great curiosity known as Soda Springs. Mixed with sugar, the water from the spring makes a drink equal to any soda prepared in Illinois. Some travelers found it a welcome distraction from the day's labors.

32

We saw this beside the trail just outside of Green River. Abigail has committed every word to memory.

Dear Abigail. We passed here July 20. Everyone well. Keep heart, we shall meet in Oregon City. Yrs Byron

INSIDE VIEW OF FORT HALL.

LEDGER

DATE:	July 27–Aug. 8
BEGINNING BALANCE:	$2,970.70
INCOME:	$0

EXPENSES:	Wagon:	$200.00
	Flour, 30 lbs.:	$15.00

CURRENT BALANCE:	$2,755.70

Dear Grandfather:

We have survived many adventures on the trail thus far. I am recording them all, and I wonder if you have seen my letters published in the newspaper. Nathan and I have spent a fortnight as ferry operators to recoup losses suffered when our cattle were stampeded. We are now rich in coin, but it is little use to us here. Fort Hall is an old boot, run down at the heel, and we are running short of supplies. We bought what little flour could be had, but it is not enough to sustain us to Oregon. What I wouldn't give for one of Mother's apple pies now. It is a hard life, but it is not comfort that has produced the great masterpieces of literature. It is good training indeed out here. I hope you will come join us when we are settled.

Yours,
William

CALIFORNIA JUNCTION

DATE: *August 13, 1852*

We reached the junction of the California Trail today, which was the occasion of much debate between the Oregonians and the gold hunters. Many farewells were said at the end of it all. One of them I will remember for the rest of my days. I was awake late in the night taking my turn as sentry when I was startled by a rustling in the sagebrush not 30 feet distant. I approached with nary a breath, expecting to be run through by a fierce arrowhead. Instead I came upon Joseph, huddled against the chill air. He did not start but told me with some trepidation that he was taking his freedom. He did not wish to dig gold for Mr. Master in California and was going to Oregon. I did not hesitate but told him to wait. I went to the wagon and returned with a buffalo hide and $50 in coin. This time he took it willingly and disappeared into the night. I returned to my duties as guard, feeling that I had done the first thing of importance in my 15 years.

Oregon-bound emigrants are held to be a better lot than the ruffians bound for the mines. It is said (falsely) that a pile of gold-bearing quartz points the way to California so as not to overwork the miner's brain.

The slave masters post ads like this one when their "property" escapes. Thanks to the Fugitive Slave Law passed two years ago, I could be jailed for helping Joseph to freedom, even though slavery is not allowed in Oregon.

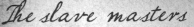

$200 Reward.

RANAWAY from the subscriber, on the night of Thursday, the 30th of September

FIVE NEGRO SLAVES,

To-wit : one Negro man, his wife, and three children. He is about forty years of age,
The man is a black negro, full bright, very erect, his face a little thin. He is probably well
and calls himself *Washington Reed*, and is known by the name of Washington. Several of his teeth
dressed, possibly takes with him an ivory headed cane, and is of good address.
are gone.
Mary, his wife, is about thirty years of age, a bright mulatto woman, and quite stout and strong.
The oldest of the children is a boy, of the name of FIELDING, twelve years of age, a dark mulatto, with
heavy eyelids. He probably wore a new cloth cap.
MATILDA, the second child, is a girl, six years of age, rather a dark mulatto, but a bright and
looking child.
MALCOLM, the youngest, is a boy, four years old, a lighter mulatto than the last, and about equally as
bright. He probably also wore a cloth cap. If examined, he will be found to have a swelling at the navel.
Washington and Mary have lived at or near St. Louis, with the subscriber, for about 15 years.
It is supposed that they are making their way to Chicago, and that a white man accompanies them, that
they will travel chiefly at night, and most probably in a covered wagon.
A reward of $150 will be paid for their apprehension, so that I can get them, if taken within one hundred
miles of St. Louis, and $200 if taken beyond that, and secured so that I can get them, and other reasonable
additional charges, if delivered to the subscriber, or to THOMAS ALLEN, Esq., at St. Louis, Mo. The
above negroes, for the last few years, have been in possession of Thomas Allen, Esq., of St. Louis.

WM. RUSSELL.

ST. LOUIS, Oct. 1, 1847.

Nathan is staying with us all the way to Oregon after being cornered by Father for some hours. Father let Nathan know, quite eloquently, that he might as well play roulette as dig for gold and that Oregon is where people make an honest living. If Father's speeches made Nathan stay, it is certainly the first time they did more than add warm breeze to the air at supper time.

THREE ISLAND CROSSING

DATE: *August 26, 1852*

Chief Washakie of the Shoshone is known to be a friend to the emigrants. He has counseled his people to keep peace with us, and we are particularly grateful tonight.

I am cold and hungry and tired, but I am alive, and for that I am in debt to an unlikely savior. It is a treacherous crossing here, a wide expanse of the Snake with a rushing current, broken by three islands. We hired three guides from the Shoshone tribe to help us ford, and all was going well until we reached the midpoint between the last island and the shore. One of the lead oxen found a hole and lost his footing. He panicked the others, and they turned abruptly downstream. Father and Nathan lay abed in the wagon, stricken by mountain fever. I did not think of the churning river but acted without thought. I plunged into the water and tried to turn the oxen back, but I too lost my footing, and the river swept me into a maelstrom. I gasped for air. The current pulled me down. The more I fought, the more the river tightened its grip, until finally I gave in and let the water take me, thinking I would come to rest either in Oregon or in God's heaven. Instead, I found myself in the embrace of one of our Shoshone guides. He dragged me ashore while his companions saved our wagon.

We traded clothing and ammunition for salmon, and it caused me to reflect upon the value we assign to our possessions. At home in Springfield, where food was plentiful, were a man to offer me a hunk of fish for my best shirt, I would have considered him a thief. Here, I consider him my savior.

A Shoshone woman taught mother a new delicacy: Herd crickets into firepits and roast them until they burst. Mash and mix with roots and herbs to make flat cakes for baking. I closed my eyes and tried to imagine apple pie.

Here is where our journey nearly ended.

August 4. Abigail, only the miles keep us apart. We are together in my heart, Byron.

Yes, another.

Grande Ronde Valley

September 12, 1852.

What a welcome sight is this valley, a true oasis in the desert. There is fine, cool water to drink and grass for the cattle.

We found some provisions here, but not many. Nathan is full of plans to purchase supplies when we arrive in Oregon and bring them back here to sell at a great profit next year.

We will not linger long here. The snowcapped peaks ahead are beautiful but warn of great danger to come if we do not hurry.

The descent from the mountains was treacherous as any we have made. We kept the wheels locked the entire way, and still we needed several men to steady each wagon with ropes.

The Indians here want for nothing. They cultivate the fields and own the finest ponies I have seen. Many have been educated by Methodist missionaries and speak tolerable English.

LEDGER

DATE:		Aug. 8–Sept. 12
BEGINNING BALANCE:		$2,755.70
INCOME:	Doctoring fees:	$16.00
	Few travelers have any money left to pay.	
EXPENSES:	Flour, 50 lbs.:	$20.00
	Beef, 20 lbs.:	$10.00
CURRENT BALANCE:		$2,741.70

THE DALLES
(CAMP DRUM)

DATE: *October 1, 1852*

I can scarcely believe it true, but the trail ends for us here. We have been four months in the barren wilds with a handful of tents, tipis, and forts posing as homes. The Dalles, or Camp Drum, as the army calls it, consists of a store, a barracks, a Catholic mission, and, miracle of miracles, HOUSES. They are little more than shacks with dirt floors, but to me they are water glimmering in the desert. I would like nothing better than to take up residence here and settle for the rest of my days. Alas, we are not through yet. Mount Hood looms like a white-crested battlement, barring the way to paradise. The women and I are strong, but Father and Nathan still suffer. We are selling the oxen (for next to nothing) and taking the Columbia—the last churning river—to our final destination.

The scurvy has taken hold, as we have not seen a berry for miles, and all dried fruit was consumed long ago. Father has treated people with his treasured pickles, and they are a miraculous cure.

And still another.

Oct. 1. Abigail, look for me in Portland city. I will wait for you there till I am old. Yours always, Byron

PICKLES

Here is how we travel the final miles to the green and golden land.

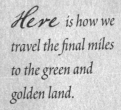

• 50 miles by raft with little current to the Cascade Falls

• 3 miles around the falls by a tramway made of timber and plank, pulled by a mule

There is a small Indian settlement here at the Dalles; Cayuse we are told. In the early days of the trail, emigrants hired them as guides. Now most people elect to go by raft through a narrow passage in the hills. Beyond lie the final miles of our journey.

• 65 miles to Portland by steamboat

PORTLAND OREGON

DATE: *October 14, 1852*

We arrived at last, and I knelt to kiss the dirt beneath my feet. Land is scarce in this city, but we have rented a log home on the outskirts of town while we search for the 640 acres we are entitled to by federal law. It is said that 10,000 people came to Oregon this year and 50,000 more to California. It will take time for them all to find homes. I do not know about the 60,000, but everyone I care for has survived the journey. There is less of each of us due to hunger. Still, as Father has said, this is a land of possibilities, and many of them have already suggested themselves to us. Hopefully there is one for Joseph in this land, though Oregon does not recognize the land claims of black men. I was moved this night to some speechifying of my own, in which I reflected on Joseph and Stannard and Byron and the legion of travelers who accompanied us westward. We are a multitude of restless souls moving heaven, earth, and a continent full of dust to better our lives. And perhaps, when our journeys reach their ultimate end, it is not what we find that matters, but the freedom to search the way we choose.

More than 1,000 people live in Portland, though it was just founded last year. It is known as "Stumptown" because people have been in such a hurry to build it that they have left stumps in the middle of the streets.

Abigail has found Byron, whose father was softened by hard times on the trail. They will marry soon and are claiming 320 acres in the Yamhill Valley. They will grow wheat to ship to California, where gold hunters supposedly pay more than $1 a pound for it.

Nathan has set himself up as a blacksmith. He has not yet made the weight of his anvil in gold, but he commands a good living repairing wagon wheels and shoeing tired horses.

LEDGER

DATE:	Sept. 12–Oct. 14
BEGINNING BALANCE:	$2,741.70
INCOME:	
Sale of oxen:	$400.00
EXPENSES:	
Steamboat, Oregon City to Portland ($5/passenger & $15 freight):	$40.00
Log home, 1 month's rent:	$80.00
CURRENT BALANCE:	$3,021.70

Thanks to Nathan, we are one of the few families that ended the journey wealthier than we were when it began.

Mother is content and making lists of the things we will need to resupply a home.

Father is recovering quickly and already tending the sick. He asks $15 from those who can pay.

And I must finally introduce a new man: *William Reed*, newspaperman. In truth, I have been hired by Mr. Thomas J. Dryer merely to sell the Weekly Oregonian. But if father approves, I will sell it eastward on the trail next year, and surely when Mr. Dryer reads my account of my adventures, he will not be able to resist.

AFTERWORD

WILLIAM REED'S OREGON TRAIL
AN AFTERWORD BY MARC ARONSON

IF I WANTED TO BE A REAL CURMUDGEON, I would start my questioning of this book with the title: the very term "Oregon Trail" is misleading. It is true that between the 1840s and the 1850s some quarter of a million people set off from the Missouri River to the West. But with so many wagons and oxen and horses and tramping feet, soon enough great stretches of the path became a roadway. Indeed there are places in the West where you can still see the ruts in the ground made by the endless passing wagons. So it was not a trail—and it didn't only lead to Oregon. Many people peeled off to California; Mormons headed to Utah; others decided to stop in Nevada, or Montana, or other parts of the West. And yet there is a way in which the term "Oregon Trail" actually has meant much more than the traces of individual Americans.

Long after people switched from wagons to railroads and then cars, the idea of the Oregon Trail remained in our minds as a symbol of new possibilities. When we think of what it means to be American, one constant image is of those who hitched up their wagons and set out to build new lives. In reality, though, the Oregon Trail brought pain as well as hope. For the Indians who saw more and more people crossing their land, the trail was a threat, not an opportunity. As the wagons kept rolling it was ever harder for the original Americans to hold on to their land and lifeways.

Young William Reed touches on all the themes I've mentioned. Yet, even though I shared this manuscript with Dr. Peter Blodgett of the Huntington Library, we could not find a single scrap of evidence to show that William, his family, the Strongs, James Marsden, or Joseph ever lived, nor is there any trace of the drawings or news dispatches William supposedly created. And yet so much of what he describes precisely matches the historical records.

More people set out on the trail in 1852 than in any other year—60,000 in all. Wagons sometimes had to ride four across, like a modern highway, to make space for all the turning wheels. With all of that traffic, there were many ways to make, or lose, money. For example, 40 different people operated ferries at 25 different river crossings. At the Elkorn River, one man reported making $500 in a single day—just as William describes at Green River. But money that came easily was easily spent. Two mountain men, who raked in $65,000 in a single summer, lost it all gambling.

While I cannot find evidence of Mr. Stannard's existence, there were scam artists just like him who preyed on the travelers. In 1851, the Mormon leader Brigham Young reported thieves at Green River trying to steal cattle using exactly the same tricks William describes. Indians sometimes helped travelers, traded with them when they could, but occasionally also fought with them. In 1853, a small group of Sioux did briefly take over a ferry, which led to a shootout with soldiers.

Families who took to the road to better themselves resented the so-called land pirates who kept finding new ways to charge tolls or otherwise separate an emigrant from his money. But even without thieves, robbers, and sharp-eyed businessmen, the trail was hard. In 1852, the year William supposedly went west, another person who kept a diary on the same trail reported seeing six graves a mile on the road to Fort Laramie. Another traveler, in 1850, counted 2,351 dead horses and mules, 433 oxen, and 787 abandoned wagons. Indeed, 1,000 people who set out that year turned around and went back home. But people also really did use the trailside to leave notes for those following behind—either warnings about hazards, or even—as Byron does—love letters.

Dr. Blodgett and I have managed to trace all of the artwork in this book that is not attributed to William, and you can find out more about those certainly authentic images on page 45. While William and his family have vanished from the historical record, this is a real history of the real Oregon Trail.

LIST OF ILLUSTRATIONS

These illustrations have been verified as historically authentic; copies can be found in museum collections and other reputable archives. Illustrations not listed here are attributed to William Reed, and, while they appear to be accurate, their historical authenticity cannot be verified.

FURTHER READING

There are many ways to learn more about the Oregon Trail, from the websites created by museums and other historical societies, to both novels and nonfiction written for nearly every age of reader. Here are some suggestions to help sort through those options.

BOOK LISTS

Parents, teachers, and librarians looking for books crafted for younger readers on a wide range of popular subjects should consult the useful guides produced by the Center for Children's Books at the University of Illinois: http://ccb.lis.uiuc.edu/bibliographies.html.

For an annotated list of books about pioneers, Lewis and Clark, and the Oregon Trail, see http://ccb.lis.uiuc.edu/bibliographies/pioneers_jan2008.html.

Another useful list from the Multnomah Library System can be found here: http://www.multcolib.org/schoolcorps/lists/Oregon_Trail_4-5.pdf.

NONFICTION

Dary, David. The *Oregon Trail: An American Saga*. Knopf, 2004. Aimed at adult general readers, it is an excellent resource for older students.

Fisher, Leonard Everett. *The Oregon Trail*. Holiday House, 1990. A solid account for middle graders, with maps, photos, and illustrations.

Greenberg, Judith D., and Helen Carey McKeever. *A Pioneer Woman's Memoir: Based on the Journal of Arabella Clemens Fulton*. Franklin Watts, 1995. One of the pleasures of researching the Oregon Trail is getting to read the memoirs of those who took the trip. This one is edited for middle grade and high school readers.

Wadsworth, Ginger. *Words West: Voices of Young Pioneers*. Clarion Books, 2003. This gives a rich sense of the lives of young people on the way west.

FICTION

Gerrard, Roy. *Wagons West!* Farrar, Straus and Giroux, 1996. This picture book gives younger elementary school students an easy entry into the story of the Oregon Trail.

Harness, Cheryl. *The Tragic Tale of Narcissa Whitman and the Faithful History of the Oregon Trail*. National Geographic Society, 2006. This is a blend of documents from the trail with new drawings and stories, aimed at middle grade readers.

ONLINE RESOURCES

Created to work with a PBS television series, this site includes a downloadable teacher's guide and has many links to explore. http://www.isu.edu/~trinmich/Oregontrail.html.

This site is organized as a lesson plan, with further links: http://edsitement.neh.gov/view_lesson_plan.asp?id=323.

This site leads to many others, including memoirs and other documents available online: http://www.endoftheoregontrail.org/histhome.html.

ENCYCLOPEDIA OF THE OREGON TRAIL

In which unusual words are defined and additional information is offered about historical figures and places mentioned in the text.

BLOOMERS: an outfit for women, consisting of a jacket, a skirt or dress that fell just below the knee, and loose-fitting pants that gathered at the ankles, as shown in the illustration at left from 1851. Designed in 1849, bloomers were popularized by magazine editor Amelia Bloomer. At the time, many people were shocked to see women wearing pants. See pages 11 and 19.

J. GOLDSBOROUGH BRUFF (1804–1889): a draftsman who worked for the U.S. government helping to prepare maps of the West. On his way to California in 1849, he wrote an account of his journey, filled with drawings of what he saw. His artwork is one of the most detailed visual records of life on the trail. See pages 15–17 and 20–21.

BUFFALO CHIPS: dried pieces of cow or buffalo dung. There are few trees in the plains, so Indians and pioneers burned buffalo chips to cook their food and keep warm. Kids had the job of collecting them when the wagon trains stopped for the night. See page 3.

CALOMEL AND LAUDANUM: two different medicines used by settlers to treat all kinds of illnesses, from diarrhea to cholera. By the 20th century, people stopped taking both because calomel, which is made from mercury, can be a dangerous poison, and laudanum, which contains alcohol and opium, is highly addictive. See page 16.

FORT LARAMIE: one of the five major forts and trading posts located along the Oregon Trail. Founded by fur traders in the 1830s, Fort Laramie was purchased by the U.S. government in 1849 and quickly became a busy stopping place where emigrants could see a blacksmith or wagon maker, buy supplies, and trade stories with other travelers. See pages 5, 18, and 44.

FUGITIVE SLAVE LAW: a law passed in 1850 that required escaped slaves be returned to their owners, even if they reached "free" states. Anyone who aided in a slave's escape would also face harsh penalties. See page 35.

GREAT AMERICAN DESERT: a geographical term used to describe the treeless plains west of the Mississippi River, once thought to be an impassable desert. As late as 1860, textbooks still labeled the region this way. See page 6.

HUMBUGGERY: nonsense. See page 16.

INDEPENDENCE ROCK: a huge granite rock formation in Wyoming. Reaching the rock before the 4th of July was thought to be a good sign for settlers trying to reach Oregon before snowfall. Sometimes known as "the Register of the Plains," the rock's surface was covered with Indian carvings and the names, initials, and messages of emigrants. See pages 5 and 20–21.

WILLIAM HENRY JACKSON (1843–1942): photographer hired by the U.S. Geological Survey to photograph the waterfalls, railroads, fur trappers, and everything else the West had to offer, shown at left in 1872. His paintings, photos, and sketches are some of the most famous images of the Oregon Trail. See pages 19 and 37.

MOUNTAIN FEVER AND SCURVY:
two of the many diseases that sickened pioneers.
Roughly 10 percent of emigrants died emigrating
to the West, and diseases were the number one
cause of death. Mountain fever most likely referred
to Rocky Mountain Spotted Fever, a deadly illness
spread by tick bites that gave people high fevers,
chills, headaches, aches, pains, and a rash. Scurvy
was a vitamin deficiency that affected travelers who
ran out of fresh fruits and vegetables. Cholera was
also a huge killer of people on the Oregon Trail. See
pages 16, 17, 36, and 40.

OREGON TRAIL: the main overland route
from the Missouri River to the Oregon Territory. The
great migration of people from the eastern United
States to the West began around 1843, although
private groups had long encouraged settlement in
Oregon (see the certificate above, circa 1831). When
gold was discovered in California in 1848, the trickle
turned into a flood. Nearly 500,000 pioneers made
the trip by covered wagon. The trail finally became
obsolete in 1869, when the completion of the
transcontinental railway made travel easier.

QUARTZ: a common mineral. Much of the gold
in California was found embedded in quartz. See
page 34.

SALERATUS: a chalky white powder similar
to baking soda. Beginning in the 1840s, saleratus
was used for cooking, mostly in making bread rise.
See page 12.

SMITHY: the workshop of a smith or blacksmith.
Smiths use tools such as heavy hammers, tongs, and
anvils to heat up metal and hammer it into tools,
horseshoes, cooking utensils, and other objects and
equipment. See pages 12 and 30.

SODA SPRINGS: natural springs of
carbonated water found in what is now Idaho. Many
emigrants stopped to rest along the Soda Springs
and enjoy the natural "soda." In 1838, a woman
named Sarah White stopped along the springs and
reported, "The water is bubbling and foaming like
boiling water. I drank of it…We find it excellent for
baking bread, no preparation of water is necessary.
Take it from the fountain & the bread is as light as
any prepared with yeast." See page 32.

ST. JOSEPH, MISSOURI: one of the
major starting points for travelers on the Oregon
Trail. St. Joe became a boomtown selling supplies
to travelers outfitting themselves for the journey
west. The city grew even larger with the addition
of the railroad. In 1860, the first rider for the Pony
Express left from St. Joseph en route to Sacramento,
California. See pages 5, 10–11, 12, and 14.

SUTLER: peddler, or seller of goods and
supplies. See page 18.

CHIEF WASHAKIE (CA 1800–1900):
chief of the Shoshone Indian tribe. Known as a
fierce warrior and a strong leader, he united his
people to fight enemy tribes such as Sioux and
Cheyennes. When wagon trains began crossing
over Shoshone land, he decided to help rather than
attack them. In 1868, he signed the Ft. Bridger
Treaty, which established a reservation for his
people in Wyoming. See page 36.

TIPI: a Native American dwelling. Tipis, such as
the one above from Oregon in 1861, were usually
made from bark, animal skins, or fabric laid over a
wooden frame. See page 40.

BRIGHAM YOUNG (1801–1877): leader
of the Mormon Church, also known as the Church of
Jesus Christ of Latter-day Saints. In 1846, Young led
about 12,000 Mormons on a "great migration" to Salt
Lake City, Utah. See pages 29 and 44.

Thank you to Dr. Peter Blodgett, Curator of Western Historical Manuscripts at the Huntington Library, for insights into the history behind William's account; to John Mark Lambertson of the National Frontier Trails Museum for confirming that William's sketch of his wagon was accurate; to Dr. Myra Zarnowski, Chair and Professor of Elementary and Early Childhood Education at Queens College, for carefully reading the entire book with modern young people in mind; and to Jane Folger of Maplewood Memorial Library for generously sharing her knowledge of children's nonfiction.

A Book by Aronson & Glenn LLC and Tod Olson LLC
Produced by Marc Aronson, John W. Glenn, and Tod Olson
Text by Tod Olson
Book design, art direction, and production by Jon Glick, mouse+tiger
Illustrations by Scott Allred and Gregory Proch
Additional research by Sarah Parvis
Copyediting by Sharon Brinkman

Published by the National Geographic Society
John M. Fahey, Jr., President and Chief Executive Officer
Gilbert M. Grosvenor, Chairman of the Board
Tim T. Kelly, President, Global Media Group
John Q. Griffin, President, Publishing
Nina D. Hoffman, Executive Vice President;
    President, Book Publishing Group

Prepared by the Book Division
Nancy Laties Feresten, Vice President, Editor in Chief, Children's Books
Bea Jackson, Director of Design and Illustrations, Children's Books
Amy Shields, Executive Editor, Series, Children's Books
Jennifer Emmett, Executive Editor, Reference and Solo, Children's Books
Carl Mehler, Director of Maps

Staff for This Book
Jennifer Emmett, Project Editor
David Seager, Art Director
Lori Epstein, Illustrations Editor
Rebecca Baines, Assistant Editor
Grace Hill, Associate Managing Editor
Lewis Bassford, Production Project Manager
Jennifer A. Thornton, Managing Editor
R. Gary Colbert, Production Director
Susan Borke, Legal and Business Affairs

Manufacturing and Quality Management
Christopher A. Liedel, Chief Financial Officer
Phillip L. Schlosser, Vice President
Chris Brown, Technical Director
Nicole Elliott, Manager

Library of Congress Cataloging-in-Publication data available upon request.

TRADE ISBN 978-1-4263-0412-5
LIBRARY ISBN 978-1-4263-0413-2

ILLUSTRATION CREDITS
Abbreviations:
SA = illustration(s) by Scott Allred
GP = illustration(s) by Gregory Proch
BL = courtesy The Bancroft Library, University of California at Berkeley
HL = courtesy The Huntington Library, San Marino, California
LOC = courtesy The Library of Congress
NYPL = courtesy The New York Public Library
OHS = courtesy The Oregon Historical Society, Portland, Oregon
SB = courtesy The Scotts Bluff National Monument, Nebraska
t = top, b = bottom, c = center, l = left, r = right

Front cover (c) and spine (b): SA; front cover (tl, tr): GP; back cover (tr): HL; back cover (cl): SB; back cover (background map, bl): LOC

Page 1 (tl, tr): GP; page 1 (b): courtesy the Walden Font Co.; page 3: GP; pages 4-5: HL; page 5 (tr): GP; page 6 (tl): GP; page 6 (tr): LOC; page 7: GP; pages 8 (tl, tr, br) and 9 (br): GP; pages 8-9 (c): LOC; pages 10-11: SA; page 12 (tl): GP; page 12 (br): Public Domain; page 13 (t): SA; page 13 (b): Public Domain; page 14 (tl, tr): GP; page 14 (b): reprinted with the permission of the People of Missouri; page 15 (all): HL; page 16 (tl): GP; page 16 (tr): HL; page 16 (bl): courtesy the National Library of Medicine; page 17 (t): LOC; page 17 (b): HL; page 18 (tl): GP; page 18 (tr): courtesy the Eiteljorg Museum of American Indians and Western Art; page 18 (b): BL; page 19 (t): GP; page 19 (b): SB; page 20 (tl): GP; pages 20 (c) and 21 (bl): HL; page 21 (br): GP; pages 22-23: SA; page 24 (tl): GP; page 24 (b): Public Domain; page 25 (all): GP; pages 26-27: SA; page 28 (all): GP; page 29 (t): NYPL; page 29 (b): LOC; pages 30 (all) and 31 (t, c): GP; page 31 (b): BL; page 32 (tl, b): GP; page 32 (tr): OHS; page 33 (t): GP; page 33 (b): HL; pages 34 (tl, bl) and 35 (c, bl): GP; page 35 (br): LOC; page 36 (tl, br): GP; page 36 (tr): LOC; page 37 (t): NYPL; page 37 (c): SB; page 37 (b): GP; pages 38-39: SA; pages 40 (tl, bl) and 41 (bl, br): GP; pages 40-41 (c): OHS; page 42 (tl): GP; page 42 (tr, br): OHS; page 43: GP; page 44: BL; page 46 (tl): LOC; page 46 (br): SB; page 47 (tl): HL; page 47 (br): LOC

Founded in 1888, the National Geographic Society is one of the largest nonprofit scientific and educational organizations in the world. It reaches more than 285 million people worldwide each month through its official journal, NATIONAL GEOGRAPHIC, and its four other magazines; the National Geographic Channel; television documentaries; radio programs; films; books; videos and DVDs; maps; and interactive media. National Geographic has funded more than 8,000 scientific research projects and supports an education program combating geographic illiteracy.

For more information, please call 1-800-NGS LINE (647-5463) or write to the following address:

National Geographic Society
1145 17th Street N.W., Washington, D.C. 20036-4688 U.S.A.

Visit us online at www.nationalgeographic.com/books

For librarians and teachers: www.ngchildrensbooks.org

More for kids from National Geographic: kids.nationalgeographic.com

For information about special discounts for bulk purchases, please contact National Geographic Books Special Sales: ngspecsales@ngs.org

For rights or permissions inquiries, please contact National Geographic Books Subsidiary Rights: ngbookrights@ngs.org

Printed in USA